As a father of two teenage sons and a church league basketball coach, I have encountered many young men who come from environments where examples are sorely needed. While I don't claim to be an expert on the subject, I do have the benefit of these 35 combined years of experience in the field as well as the benefit of having had a number of mentors who passed along "man wisdom" during that critical time. This book is designed to create a baseline of behavior for young men to indoctrinate into their daily lives as well as help single moms shore up the void of an absentee father. This is a do-it-yourself guide sprinkled with a bit of anecdotal humor. So, without any further ado, I humbly present: The 10 ComMANdments of Manhood.

"It is easier to build boys than to repair broken men"- Frederick Douglass (modified)

Dedication

This book is dedicated to several people who have helped make this revelation a reality: my brother Austin, whose listening ear and sage advice gave clarity and simplicity to this project; my sons, Michael and Markous, whose experiences are, to some extent, the undercurrent of the book; the countless number of young men that I had the pleasure of coaching and mentoring, and, last but not least, my wife, Michele. I've told you over the years that you married a "mad scientist" and that I know how hard that is! Thanks for your unyielding support and love of a man who can be difficult to understand pretty darn often; I love you more than I can ever express!

Table of Contents

I.	"Man Up:" What does it mean?

Learning to "Boy Up" Before You "Man Up"

This concept is probably the most perplexing one for young men to deal with: "Man Up." This issue is compounded by the fact that quite often the phrase is coming from a woman! It's almost as if there's supposed to be a switch that is magically activated when "Man Up!" is heard! May I share something with you? Telling a 7-, 10-, 13-, 15- or 17-year-old boy to "Man Up" will NOT make it happen! What does that mean? How do I do it?

Here's a working definition: "Man Up" simply means to take personal responsibility for (own) every mistake you make as well as tackle your problems head-on. In a purely physical sense, it refers to applying strength to move or carry something. This concept has become a mystical one due to a convergence of factors, not the least of which is my generation's failure to reach back and teach these young men this very simple yet profound principle. Unfortunately, if you were born in or after 1965, there is a very good chance that you saw or were a product of a broken home and, by extension, didn't see your dad in the home showing you what manhood should look like. When you add to that, the Feminist movement being in full swing in the 1970s, what you have is a situation that lends itself to boys "falling through the cracks" in terms of getting the much-needed guidance that a man is best at giving. Don't get me wrong: I am not here to "blame Eve" for the male societal ills, but it is an unfortunate reality nonetheless.

Let's talk about "Boy Up" for a sec. The term came about around 10 years ago while I was coaching my oldest son's little league football team. As I looked around, I noticed that there were a number of single moms watching practice and complaining about why their sons had to work so hard. My first thoughts were rather unflattering, but then as I thought about and watched these boys ask the same question, I had an epiphany: unless a boy learns to embrace the idea of having to deal with "hardships" (CHALLENGES), early life becomes a series of failure after failure, each perpetuated by some "reason" (EXCUSE) that shirk the concept of personal responsibility. In plain English, "Boy Up" simply means to face all challenges (academic, social, athletic) head-on and take responsibility for your mistakes.

"Man Up." That simply means that, as men, we must OYS (or OYI, depending on your linguistic tilt) aka Own Your Ish!! Your mistakes belong to YOU; no one made you do it!! I believe that if we can teach these boys this concept, we can begin to curb and ultimately reverse the damage done by absent dads and well-meaning, but completely unaware, moms. This is, far and away, THE MOST IMPORTANT ComMANdment OF THE 10 ComMANdments OF MANHOOD! If we fail to implement this, everything else will fail miserably.

II.	Eye Contact

<u>Always Look a Man in the Eye When Having a Conversation</u>

This is a staple of respectful interaction with people; but when dealing with building young men, it can't be stressed enough.	There is an epidemic of society having become fundamentally rude while simultaneously trying to maintain some semblance of political correctness. I see this cultural collision daily whenever I see boys being addressed by men. It is almost as if they are afraid to do so! However, as I began to delve into this particular phenomenon, I realize that this is very closely related to the premise of "Man Up." I'm not sure that I give someone my full attention if he isn't looking me in the eye. Eye contact should be strong but not uncomfortable. Over the years, I struggle with how much eye contact is normal. Research indicates that holding eye contact for 3-5 seconds at a time is appropriate. This sign of respect is based on a very basic premise: who among us wants to be ignored when interacting with others? I realize that this generation is "socially challenged" due to the advent of social media, but this has got to stop! This both gives and commands respect; it gives the person you happen to be in front of his or her due attention and it subtly demands the same in return. Eye contact also does something that millions of words, no matter how eloquently delivered, cannot replicate: trust. We tend to deem someone as trustworthy or not, based on this little thing. According to forensic psychology, one's honesty is determined by certain involuntary motions, eye contact being on that list. The man who is able to maintain eye contact is more likely to build a rapport than he who is unable to. Once mastered, you can fully develop an aura that commands respect … #themanhoodmovement

III.   How to Shake Hands

Give a firm grip when shaking hands. If I had a dollar for every time some young cat gave me the "limp fish" grip, I could take a couple of weeks off from work! You get ONE initial impression and a grip, especially when introducing yourself to another man, sets the stage for how you will be perceived by him going forward. This is an easy fix; just make it a point to "let him know you're there" and proceed accordingly ... #themanhoodmovement

IV.   Posture!

What is this? Posture is simply the way you sit and/or stand. Movie stars and models have mastered this little thing that goes really far when it comes to projecting confidence. Again, as I harken back to days gone by, one of the things that made you notice a man was the way he sat and stood: upright, tall, commanding! Another easy fix: make it a habit to sit up straight (you know, like your mother and grandmother used to make you do). Once you become comfortable with this, add a walk that reflects these same habits and now you're on to something! Many a woman has made a remark about how some man carried himself; that referred to his posture and walk. What this generation calls "swag" is actually your version of a certain style that men once possessed but seems to be lost today. My wife, like so many millions of women, is a huge fan of Denzel Washington. One of the things that seems to be consistently attractive to his female fans is his walk. While I'm not a fan of imitating another man's style, I can agree that developing a similar posture and walk can make you feel confident even when you're not! Part of the "fake it till you make it" can be found in selling an appearance to others. I'm not encouraging anyone to be dishonest; however, I do believe that "manufactured confidence" is merely a method of finding the courage to move forward when your feet have clearly given up …

#themanhoodmovement

V.   Speak Clearly!

The perception of manhood can be changed by the implementation of a host of little things. One of those "little things" is being able to speak clearly. While I get that this generation is filled with "mumblers" (rappers who do this...way too many acts to name) that doesn't fly out here in the real world. Once upon a time a man used his voice and words to make his presence felt; nowadays there isn't a discernible difference between men and boys in this regard! We've all heard the old saying, "You never get a second chance to make a first impression," right? An easy yet effective way to leave someone with a positive impression of you is to speak clearly and to practice Standard English when addressing others. I get it; we live in a "microwave society" but some things are and should not change. Many of us have a nasty habit of using slang when we talk (excuse me, TEXT) to others (co-workers, teachers/supervisors) and it poisons all of our speech habits. Things like "Ikr," "Ijs," "Wyd," and "Idk" have effectively killed the practice of full words and sentences. Admittedly, I am guilty of many of these things as well, but I still put complete sentences to use; Ijs (sorry; couldn't resist).

My point is this: Usage of complete sentences on a regular basis allows you to get more things done because while it may feel like time wasted, you get it back in the form of not having to explain what you mean by some popular slang phrases ... #themanhoodmovement

VI.   Humble Confidence

Be humbly confident! Your confidence should be rooted in your abilities, but be humble enough to know that you didn't develop them on your own. Let me be clear: confidence doesn't necessarily mean having a "street edge;" you simply, in the words of many of my elders when trying to define faith, "act as if." Act as if you deserve that job, that date, etc. If you lack it, manufacture it, aka "fake it till you make it." Confidence, like many other things, is born in the mind by a single thought or mantra being repeated until it takes root. The 5th ComMANdment alludes to "faith;" confidence is her soulmate! When confidence and faith intersect, their union will produce a baby named "success" - Michael Bryant … #themanhoodmovement

VII.   Go to Work

This is a staple of universal manhood. In fact, it is the true constant of male life from pre-school until death! Here's the scoop, "work" is the essence of what men do, period! As boys, we learn to "work" when we have to go to "practice" for a sport or playing an instrument. For those of us who aren't athletically inclined, this includes homework or extra-curricular activities, i.e., chess club, debate team, etc. The point here is that there is always something for a man to pour his time into. "Work" serves as a metaphor for any and all things that require an investment of time and repetition. I have told my sons (repeatedly) that there are two (2) things that you must remember: 1) I love you more than you will ever know, and 2) men go to work! "Work" also refers to any chores assigned to you at home as well as entrepreneurial pursuits. Please understand that no forward progress can be made without applying   this   profoundly   simple   premise   … #themanhoodmovement

VIII.   Financial Responsibility

Be financially responsible! Far too many of us take this for granted. While "going to work" is good, we need to be able to address life's "surprises" when they arise (and they will). Put a little bit aside (10% minimum) to avoid throwing yourself into full-on chaos. Also, pay your bills on time! The men that came before us understood that credit is often used as a character measure. This isn't necessarily a "man thing" per se, but it is something that can and will make your life easier. There are lots of resources that can give you a good running start with this ComMANdment. I won't give the names of any here, but please believe that this will come in handy sooner than later. We, as men, sometimes overlook this fact of life. We see this financial irresponsibility show among athletes and entertainers pretty often and find ourselves wondering how people who make lots of money can have the same problems that you and I have. Here's where it starts. The act of living below your means requires a good bit of discipline, but the payoff will be well worth the sacrifice. I have finally figured out that I can have more money than month just by doing this simple thing ... #themanhoodmovement

IX.   Executable Life Plan

Have an executable plan and follow it! We expect women to follow and dudes to respect us but it isn't reasonable without, at bare minimum, a vision. You gotta know what you want in order to get yourself aligned with it. Please trust me on this: it only took me over 40 years to figure out that all those people who told me this were right! Planning has a spiritual connotation as well: the word "faith" is defined as "the substance of things hoped for, the evidence of things not seen." If you are a practicing Christian, Muslim, Jew or New Ageist, you should already have an understanding of the necessity of planning. If you're an agnostic or atheist, you REALLY know how important it is to plan! Regardless of your belief system (or absence of one) a plan is the roadmap to success. Please be mindful that your success may not match others' definition but, only YOU can determine what success means to YOU! Do yourself a favor: take this at face value and save yourself some unnecessary hardship … #themanhoodmovement

X.	Study/Read/Research!

No one talks about this enough. This doesn't involve anything "cool" but it will pay dividends long after being "cool" is an afterthought. In the eye of many, Barack Obama is the "coolest" POTUS (President of the United States) ever. Some may not know that the former POTUS is a Harvard Law School graduate who is actually a self-professed "geek" who enjoys Star Trek and collected comic books as a kid. Why is this important? Because as "cool" as he is in public it took years of school (READ: studying, reading and researching) to get to the point where it served him well. His "SRR" refers to Columbia University and Harvard Law School; his reward became the presidency. While most of us may not have such lofty aspirations, the formula he used is a universal one: in all pursuits study/read/research then apply what you learn until you achieve your goal! Many of us (my hand is raised) get a bit ahead of ourselves and neglect to complete this part of pursuing a goal because "we think we have it all figured out." We forget that success generally comes AFTER preparation and that preparation generally involves SRR to completion (certificate, degree, etc.). I believe that in an era where information is so readily available the value of a college degree is rising due to what that degree represents: the ability to start and complete a long-term task. Not many graduate in the "standard" 4 years for any number of reasons, i.e. "life happening" (unexpected additions to family, job status, sometimes just frustration) but for those who do, the reward is indescribable, I'm sure! Unfortunately, I fall into the group that started and failed to finish, which serves as a glaring example of why SRR + application = success. The lesson here is this: we control our individual successes and failures by the simple yet challenging approach of SRR + application. Stay the course; it will pay off. This is an extension of the "Executable Life Plan" ComMANdment, merely applied. Application of this equals to clarity on how to pursue your dreams … #themanhoodmovement

XI.   Watch Your Circle!

This is an underrated part of manhood: the part where WHO you hang around determines HOW you are perceived. Future, a famous Atlanta-based rapper had a song called, "Squares Out Your Circle." The premise of this song is basically to watch who you let get close to you because betrayal is real. While I can't speak to his motivation for said lyrics, I can definitely relate to that concept! Peer pressure is hard on adults but especially hard on kids, in particular teens. Why is this important? Association brings on assimilation. Simply put: each of us is the sum total of the 5 people we spend the most time with and around. Each of us has the power to influence and be influenced; the only question is which role do we play? Many people say that we are all born to lead but I'm not sure about that. What I mean is that while I agree that we should all seek "the truth:" my "truth" and your "truth" may not be the same. Not only that, but they may be opposing truths that can't be paired up and compromised. The beautiful thing about life is that whatever path you CHOOSE you will find others heading in the same direction. The problem with this is someone has to make the sound decisions for the group. In this regard, being the "voice of reason" can be a really good thing! This is where receiving good wholesome instructions comes into play. The instructions you receive directly determine how you respond when challenges arise; thus, comes the necessity of choosing your friends carefully. As much as teens struggle with this, the "elephant in the room" regarding this is the twenty-somethings (millennials) who find themselves caught up in regrettable situations as a result of poor friend/associate choices. To the teens I say, "Your parents don't usually miss on what they see in your choices." To the millennials I say, "Nothing is a secret anymore; social media will record and preserve your indiscretions forever!" There's nothing cool about what has been written here but it is the TRUTH! … #themanhoodmovement

XII   The Strength of Apology

Learn to apologize when you're wrong! No one wants to be wrong (EVER), but growth only occurs after the pain of mistakes is acknowledged. If you're anything like me (and I'm sure you are) there is no worse feeling than being wrong, especially when I was loud and arrogant about it. The African-American barber shop is the place where many of us learn how to argue (read: LOUD but not necessarily RIGHT) and we unknowingly carry these habits into other interactions, i.e., relationships, and it doesn't help matters any! It's particularly hard in a romantic relationship. I mean, here you are trying to gain an advantage (the alleged "upper hand") and you have to go back and try to undo what was done! Sucks, doesn't it? The greatest gains happen when you are able to "put pride aside" and simply own your transgression!! Does this sound familiar? It should! This is merely an example of "Man Up" applied. Think about it: owning a mistake effectively takes away most of the "I told you so" dialogue that far too many of us find ourselves caught up in (there will still be some but a whole lot less). I am guilty of many things, but I'm glad to say that this one doesn't rear its ugly head very often; my prayer is that my readers will learn this lesson decades before I did … #themanhoodmovement

XIII. Dealing with Emotions

Deal with your emotions! This might be a bit touchy because of how it sounds, but think about it: how many times have we all witnessed dudes "feeling some type of way" or "getting in their feelings" and doing something that they later regret? I'm gonna go out on a limb and say that we've all been there; perhaps this is avoided by learning how to correctly process our emotions. Let's start here: You are allowed to have these moments.as they are a part of the human experience. Many of us have been taught that feeling emotional is "soft," "ladylike" and "just not what men do." There is a time to be stoic but it's unhealthy to try to bottle up or ignore your emotions. Denying them leads to bad decisions because those emotions lead to lapses in judgment, some of which are infamous. In 1999 a horrific incident took place in Columbine, Colorado where two teenage boys killed 15 students and injured 21 others at Columbine High School, ultimately due to excessive bullying by their classmates. To say that this was just a matter of "not being able to process your emotions" is oversimplified; however, it did contribute to this very unfortunate situation taking place. While this is a very extreme example of lack of proper emotional processing it does serve as a reminder of just how necessary this ComMANdment is. Every boy needs a place where he can go and process these things in a healthy manner. I've created a "safe zone" in our home for our sons to let their emotions loose without judgment. The goal, of course, is emptying yourself of poisonous feelings before they spread; it appears to be working. Men need to know that it's not only ok but normal to have feelings. This should cut down on the "bad decision" dynamic that many of us have experienced in our lives … #themanhoodmovement

XIV.   Relationship Preparation

Fix yourself before jumping into a relationship! I can write a book (literally) on this: get in a relationship, it goes sideways and you break up, then find yourself in a rebound relationship with a good person but wind up dogging that person out or not being fully invested. We dudes are usually pretty slow about revealing feelings for 2 basic reasons: 1) we don't trust easily and/or 2) we aren't quick to want to give up control. This era is different from any other because there are just as many women openly "gaming" as there are men. As a result, the mantra "trust no one" seems to have permeated our society completely. There goes trust; well, until you find someone trustworthy. Let's face it: a relationship can't be fully functional unless both parties are willing to give up a significant amount of control. When you're "gaming," you can't always see a "good thing" when it comes along; if you've been "gamed," the "good thing" you see will probably be obscured by your desire to get your "pound of flesh." Neither scenario ends well, so it's best to take a step back and regroup before jumping into a relationship. Give yourself 6 months (minimum) to process and work through all residual feelings then see what's out there for you. You'll avoid the, "You need to let go of that @#$%&," conversation …

#themanhoodmovement

XV.   Plain Dealing with Women

Make your intentions plain when dealing with women. Far too many of us dudes have lied and/or led women to believe something that was nowhere near the ultimate agenda (my hand is raised). You might be surprised at the number of women who already see through the smoke screen. Here's the deal: women are smarter than us! You know that, right? If you know that, then you know that by the time you think of it, she already has, believe me! I always considered myself to be a smooth talker (and one of the 315 smartest men on Earth) but found myself humbled when talking to my future wife. I'm on some "I got game" type ish when she says something along the lines of, "You know I know what you have up your sleeve, right?" Of course, I tried to play it off but she gave me chapter and verse. I stepped back (reluctantly) and owned my not-so-hidden agenda. Little did I know that she had laid it out; all I had to do was not mess it up! Conventional wisdom says that a woman immediately knows whether or not the man that approaches her has a legitimate shot, so my now-wife's reaction brought this revelation home to me in a profound way. The lesson is this: Honesty is the best policy, and to quote the esteemed

Negro poet/philosopher, Andre 3000: "Have you ever heard of a player with no game? Told the truth to get what I want but shot it with no shame" … #themanhoodmovement.

Conclusion

To wrap it up, there are 10 things (ComMANdments) that, if applied, instantly thrust you into the throes of manhood fully prepared:

I.   "Man Up"

II.   Eye Contact

III.   How to Shake Hands

IV.   Posture!

V.   Speak Clearly

VI.   Humble Confidence

VII.   Go to Work

VIII.   Financial Responsibility

IX.   Executable Life Plan

X.   Study/Read/Research!

XI.   Watch Your Circle!

XII.   The Strength of Apology

XIII.   Dealing with Emotions

XIV.   Relationship Preparation

XV.   Plain Dealing with Women

I'm not an expert on manhood; what I can tell you is what NOT to do. Unfortunately, many of these lessons were lost on me because I was too embarrassed/prideful to ask for help, not to mention I acted as if I should have understood how manhood works (or what it is for that matter) at 21. My aim is to steer as many of you away from these fallacious mental approaches as possible. Always, ALWAYS seek guidance when questions or unfamiliar situations occur! Add this to the above-listed ComMANdments and man life becomes a much easier task to manage ... #themanhoodmovement

P.S. -- I'm sure that have you noticed the ComMANdments listed and discovered that there are more than 10. This is my gift to you. In southern Louisiana, this is called, "lagniappe." It means an unexpected or extra benefit: a bonus!

Registered this 25th day of July 2017.